ALL–STAR
SMACK>>>
>>DOWN

CONNOR McDAVID
vs. MARIO LEMIEUX

WHO WOULD WIN?

K.C. KELLEY

Lerner Publications ◆ Minneapolis

SPORTS THRILLS *MEET* **RESEARCH SKILLS**

Lerner **SPORTS**

Free Database Trial: **lernersports.com**

Lerner Publications Company
An imprint of Lerner Publishing Group, Inc.
241 First Avenue North
Minneapolis, MN 55401 USA

For reading levels and more information, look up this title at www.lernerbooks.com.

Main body text set in Aptifer Sans LT Pro.
Typeface provided by Linotype AG.

Library of Congress Cataloging-in-Publication Data

Names: Kelley, K. C., author.
Title: Connor McDavid vs Mario Lemieux : who would win? / K.C. Kelley.
Other titles: Connor McDavid versus Mario Lemieux
Description: Minneapolis, MN : Lerner Publications, [2024] | Series: All-star smackdown | Includes bibliographical references and index. | Audience: Ages 7–11 years | Audience: Grades 4–6 | Summary: "Connor McDavid and Mario Lemieux have both dominated the NHL from the center position. But which hockey superstar is better? Explore their careers and choose a winner"— Provided by publisher.
Identifiers: LCCN 2023034664 (print) | LCCN 2023034665 (ebook) | ISBN 9798765625866 (library binding) | ISBN 9798765628102 (paperback) | ISBN 9798765632048 (epub)
Subjects: LCSH: Hockey players—Rating of—Juvenile literature. | Hockey players—Statistics—Juvenile literature. | McDavid, Connor, 1997-—Juvenile literature. | Lemieux, Mario, 1965-—Juvenile literature. | National Hockey League—Juvenile literature.
Classification: LCC GV847.25 .K455 2024 (print) | LCC GV847.25 (ebook) | DDC 796.962092/2—dc23/eng/20231122

LC record available at https://lccn.loc.gov/2023034664
LC ebook record available at https://lccn.loc.gov/2023034665

Manufactured in the United States of America
1 – CG – 7/15/24

TABLE OF CONTENTS

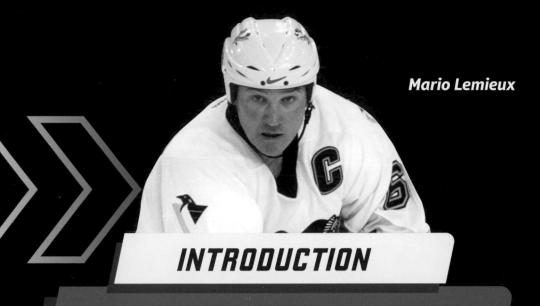

Mario Lemieux

INTRODUCTION

TWO HOCKEY STARS

Pittsburgh Penguins fans were thrilled on December 27, 2000. Skating onto the ice was a familiar player wearing jersey number 66. It was Mario Lemieux! He had gone through cancer treatments in 1993. A few seasons later, he retired from the National Hockey League (NHL). What was he back doing on the ice?

 Fast Facts

- ✪ Mario Lemieux led the Pittsburgh Penguins to two Stanley Cups.
- ✪ Lemieux won six NHL scoring titles.
- ✪ Connor McDavid has won five NHL scoring titles.
- ✪ McDavid is the sixth NHL player to reach 150 points in a season.

Lemieux was a superstar who was on his way to the Hockey Hall of Fame. He had even become a co-owner of the Penguins after retiring from the team in 1997. But he missed playing. He wanted his four young kids to see him play. So Lemieux trained in secret for months before returning. He had two assists and a goal in his first game back!

Lemieux's comeback is just part of his amazing story. He won six NHL scoring titles and led the Pittsburgh Penguins to two Stanley Cup championships. He was one of the best all-around players ever.

Connor McDavid is another hockey superstar who uses his talent to lead his team to victories. McDavid has long been a top player. By the age of six, he was playing better than the nine-year-olds in his league. In 2015, McDavid reached the NHL with the Edmonton Oilers. The next season, he was the NHL scoring champ at only 20 years old.

Like Lemieux, McDavid plays center and is a top goal scorer. McDavid won five NHL scoring titles in his first eight seasons. It took Lemieux 11 seasons to do that. Few players can skate faster than McDavid. He has an amazing ability to score from just about anywhere.

Which player is better? That's up to you to decide. Let the smackdown begin!

McDavid (left) has great stickhandling skills.

One of McDavid's best skills is his skating speed.

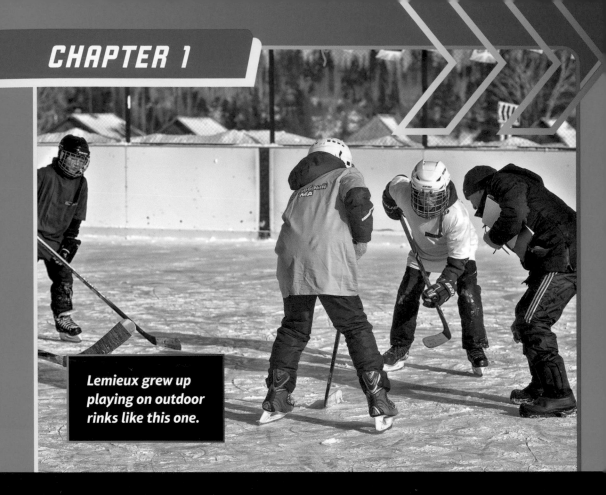

CHAPTER 1

Lemieux grew up playing on outdoor rinks like this one.

THE ROAD TO THE NHL

Mario Lemieux was born October 5, 1965, in Montréal, Quebec, Canada. Hockey is huge in Quebec. Mario got his first skates when he was only three. He loved playing with his two brothers in the family's front-yard rink. When they couldn't play outside, they whacked a ball around the kitchen with wooden spoons. Mario began playing in leagues with older kids.

When he was 15, Lemieux joined the Laval Voisins of the Major Junior League. In 1980, he set a new single-season record with 133 goals in 70 games. In three seasons, he banged in 247 goals.

Lemieux was clearly one of the best young players in the world. The Pittsburgh Penguins chose him number-one overall in the 1984 NHL Draft. Lemieux wasted no time showing what he could do. He scored a goal on his first NHL shot! He went on to score 100 points that season. Lemieux won the Calder Memorial Trophy as the NHL's top rookie.

Lemieux (center) always drew a lot of attention from defenders.

Lemieux's shots were so strong that his stick bent as he whipped the puck toward the goal.

Lemieux was big and strong, and he was also fast. He could even stickhandle like a superstar. His size and skill made him hard to stop. In 1987–1988, he was the NHL scoring champ with an incredible 168 points.

In 1988–1989, Lemieux had one of the greatest seasons in hockey history. He had career highs with 85 goals and 114 assists. His total of 199 points is fifth most all-time.

He missed much of the 1990–1991 season because of back surgery. But Lemieux worked hard to return for the playoffs. Often in great pain, he still led his team with 44 points. Only Wayne Gretzky has scored more points in a postseason. The Penguins beat the Minnesota North Stars to win their first Stanley Cup. They won it again in 1992.

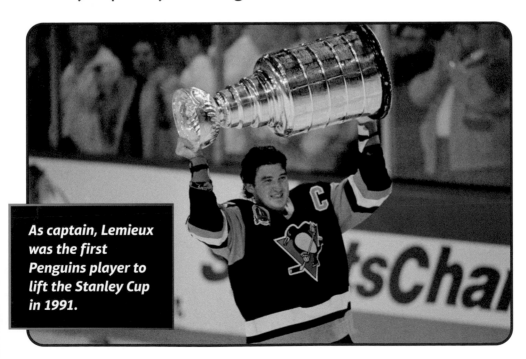

As captain, Lemieux was the first Penguins player to lift the Stanley Cup in 1991.

CONSIDER THIS

For a class project, Connor McDavid made a video about the career of another Canadian hockey star, Sidney Crosby. Like Connor, Crosby was a young superstar who became a top NHL scorer.

Connor McDavid was born January 13, 1997, near Toronto, Ontario, Canada. Like Lemieux, he was skating by the age of three. By the time Connor was 10, he was the biggest thing in Canadian youth hockey.

When Connor was in seventh grade, his parents moved him to Premier Elite Athletes Collegiate (PEAC). This Toronto school combined high-level sports with schoolwork. Even among other top players, Connor was the best. He scored six goals in one of his first games at PEAC.

What makes him so good? He has speed and shooting skill. But his special talent is how well he knows the game. Coaches call it "hockey smarts," and McDavid has more than just about any other player.

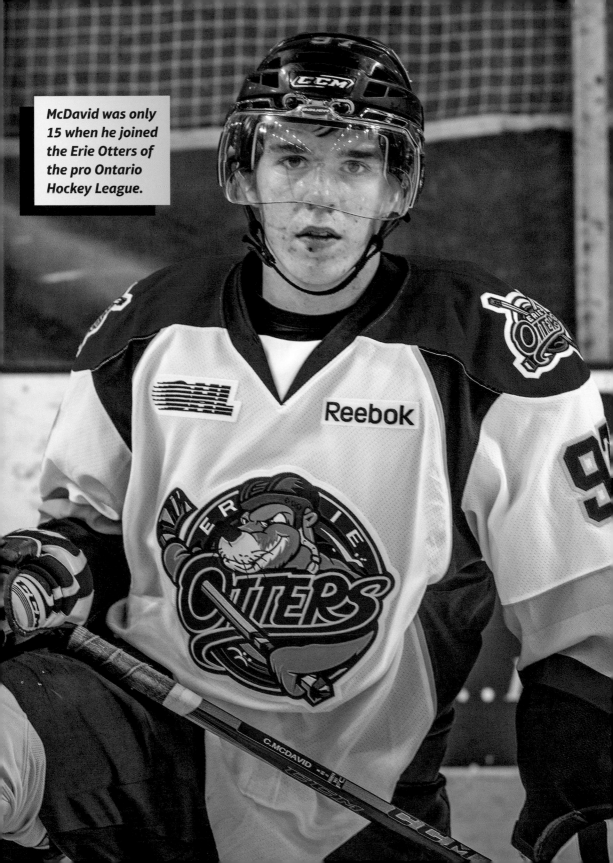

McDavid was only 15 when he joined the Erie Otters of the pro Ontario Hockey League.

McDavid joined the pro Ontario Hockey League when he was 15. The Erie Otters made him the first draft pick in 2012. He had to live about 75 miles (121 km) away from home. He played three years for the Otters. In his last season, he scored 120 points in just 47 games.

The Edmonton Oilers chose McDavid first overall in the 2015 NHL Draft. He was already so famous that he filmed several TV ads before his first NHL game. In his second season, he was the top scorer in the league. There was a lot more to come.

As the top draft pick, McDavid was often in the media spotlight.

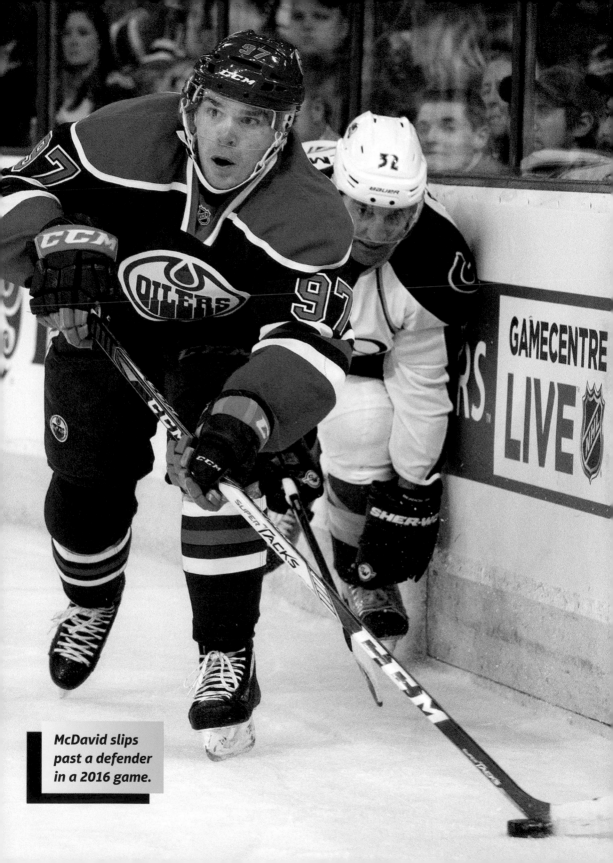

McDavid slips
past a defender
in a 2016 game.

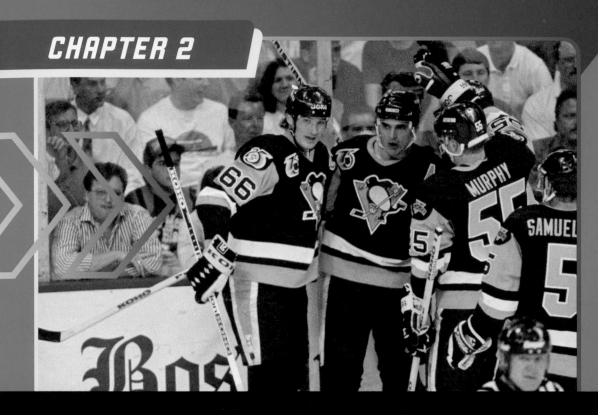

CHAPTER 2

GREATEST MOMENTS

Lemieux always battled injuries. He suffered a broken hand. He had two back surgeries. He had trouble with his hip. But he was a tough hockey player. He kept fighting to return to help his team. But in early 1993, he faced his biggest challenge.

Lemieux was on his way to breaking the NHL single-season scoring record. In January, he shocked fans when he told them he had a type of cancer called Hodgkin's disease. Lemieux had to leave the team for two months for treatment.

Lemieux went through cancer treatment that made him feel sick and weak. He watched his team on TV from home and the hospital.

Finally, the treatments ended on March 2. Lemieux was free of cancer. He returned to the Penguins that night. He went on to win the scoring title with 160 points in just 60 games. He was the MVP again. The league also gave him a special award for the courage he showed by coming back.

Lemieux (left) takes a shot during a 1993 game after his return to the ice.

McDavid was only 20 years old when he won his first NHL scoring title. He led the league with 70 assists. His 30 goals pushed him up to 100 points, topping all other players. He was living up to the promise he showed as a young player. He was the third-youngest player to win the Hart Memorial Trophy, the NHL's MVP award.

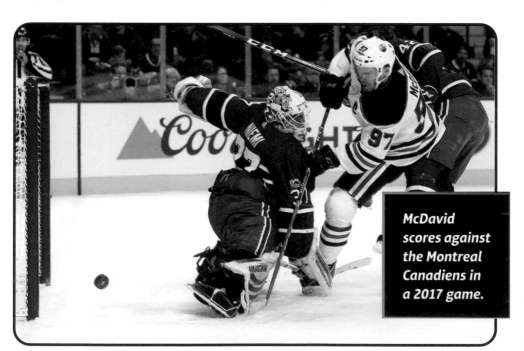

McDavid scores against the Montreal Canadiens in a 2017 game.

Scoring goals is great. But winning games is better. In 2021–2022, McDavid was the scoring champ again. He even finished second in the voting for NHL MVP. But he wanted team success too.

McDavid led the Oilers to the playoffs for the fourth time. They beat the Los Angeles Kings and then the Calgary Flames. Though the team lost to the Colorado Avalanche in the next round, McDavid's 33 playoff points were the most that season. It was the farthest McDavid had taken his team so far.

Calgary fans were not happy when McDavid (right) and the Oilers beat the Flames in the 2022 playoffs.

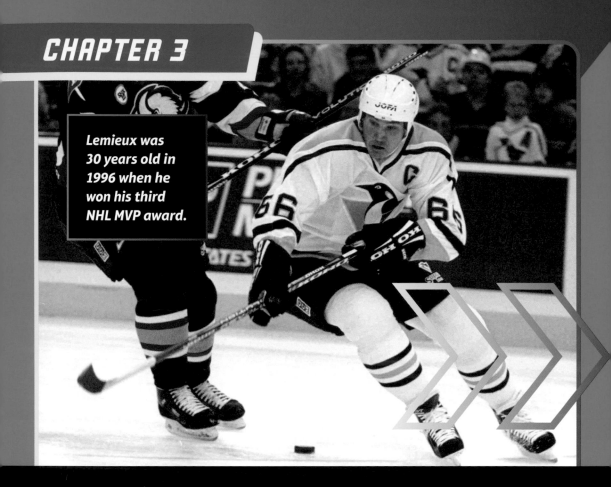

CHAPTER 3

Lemieux was 30 years old in 1996 when he won his third NHL MVP award.

RECORD-SETTING SEASONS

Lemieux missed most of the 1993–1994 season with a back injury. He scored only 37 points. The Penguins lost early in the playoffs. Even worse, he had to miss the entire 1994–1995 season. But Lemieux didn't give up. He worked out every day to help his back heal. The hard work paid off. In 1995–1996, he again led the NHL in goals, assists, and points. He won his third NHL MVP award.

In 1997, Lemieux faced another serious health problem. Doctors said he had a problem with his heart. For his safety, he retired from the sport. He was soon elected to the Hockey Hall of Fame. In 1999, he helped prevent the Penguins from leaving Pittsburgh by becoming a co-owner of the team. It seemed the rest of his hockey life would be in an office, not on the ice. But Lemieux had other ideas.

By 2000 his heart problem had improved, and he returned to the Penguins. He played five more seasons. He no longer played like a superstar, but he was a veteran leader. In 2002, he helped Canada win the gold medal at the Olympic Games in Salt Lake City, Utah.

After winning the gold medal, Lemieux carries the Canadian flag.

CONSIDER THIS

Both Lemieux and McDavid piled on the points. Lemieux averaged 1.88 points per game in his career. McDavid has averaged 1.53 points.

Connor McDavid's shocking stats just keep growing. He began 2022–2023 with a rush of goals and assists. He had two hat tricks in the Oilers' first eight games. Using his great speed and hockey smarts, he scored goal after goal. His teammates were getting perfect passes from McDavid too. He reached 35 points in only 20 games!

On April 1, 2023, the Oilers earned a spot in the playoffs. But McDavid kept piling up points. On April 8, he got two goals and an assist, giving him 151 points. He finished the season with 153.

No one had scored 150 points since the 1995–1996 season, when Lemieux had 161. McDavid is only the sixth player in NHL history to reach 150 points. And for the first time, he led the entire league in goals with 64.

Only Wayne Gretzky, Lemieux, and Steve Yzerman have scored more points in a season than McDavid's 153 in 2022–2023.

CHAPTER 4

As Penguins co-owner, Lemieux (right) *helped the team acquire their next big superstar,* Sidney Crosby (left).

AND THE WINNER IS

In this NHL all-star smackdown, who comes out on top? You can decide for yourself. Since McDavid came into the NHL, people have debated if he is better than Lemieux. That's part of the fun of being a hockey fan!

Lemieux owns many NHL records and is Pittsburgh's all-time scoring leader. Even after retiring from playing, he remains a big part of the game. Though he sold his part of the Penguins in 2021, he still helps run the team. He also started a foundation that raises millions of dollars to help fight cancer.

McDavid has played about half as many seasons as Lemieux did, but he has proven to be Lemieux's equal in many ways. In 2023, McDavid earned his third Hart Memorial Trophy. Lemieux won the same number of NHL MVP awards. Does McDavid have more in store for Edmonton fans?

McDavid's speed separates him from other players. It could help him top Lemieux's stats one day. Lemieux played 17 seasons at a high level. Can McDavid stick around long enough to match Super Mario?

In 2022–2023, McDavid won trophies as the NHL's top scorer, MVP, and most outstanding player.

McDavid might someday beat Lemieux's records. He certainly has the skills to do it. But can he avoid injuries? Will his teammates be enough to help him win? He's a fantastic player, but he needs help and luck to top Lemieux.

Lemieux is one of the top-scoring players ever. He's in the top 10 all-time in both goals and points. He battled back from injuries and cancer. He's a Hall of Famer, a hockey legend, and the winner of this smackdown. Who do you think the winner is? Look at the stats and make your own choice!

When McDavid has the puck on his stick, he is the most dangerous player in the NHL.

Lemieux put on his number 66 jersey at a 2016 event honoring the 1992 Stanley Cup-winning Penguins.

SMACKDOWN BREAKDOWN

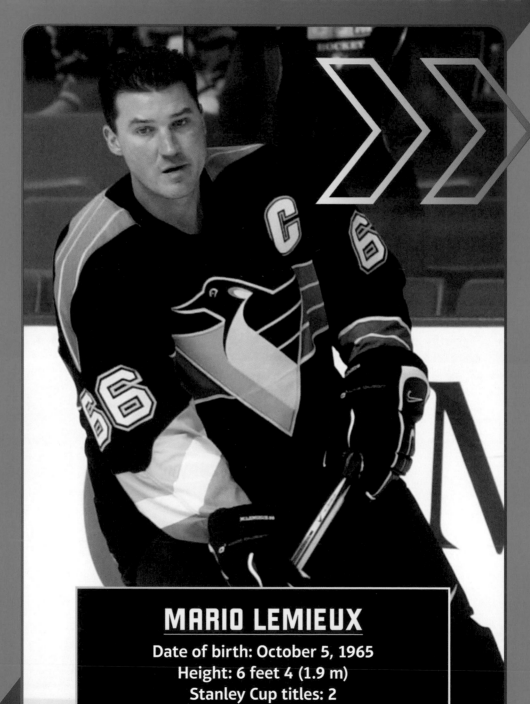

MARIO LEMIEUX

Date of birth: October 5, 1965
Height: 6 feet 4 (1.9 m)
Stanley Cup titles: 2
NHL All-Star Games: 10
NHL scoring titles: 6

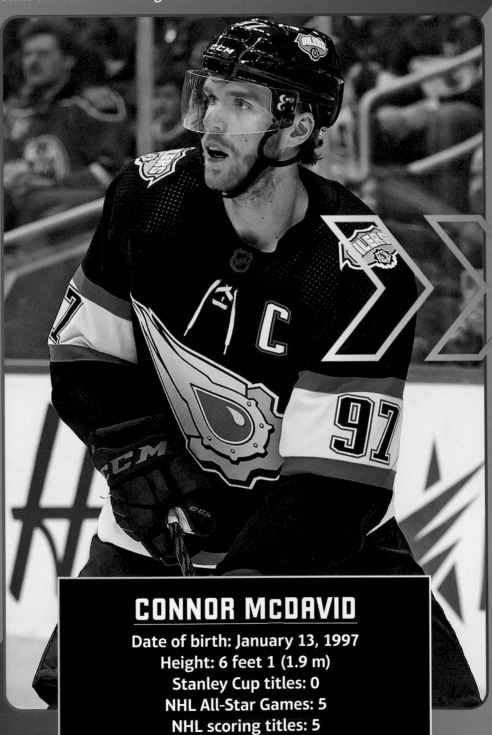

CONNOR McDAVID

Date of birth: January 13, 1997
Height: 6 feet 1 (1.9 m)
Stanley Cup titles: 0
NHL All-Star Games: 5
NHL scoring titles: 5

GLOSSARY

assist: a pass from a teammate that leads to a goal

center: a player who usually plays in the middle of the ice

conference: one of a group of teams that make up a league. The NHL has two conferences, the Eastern Conference and the Western Conference.

draft: when teams take turns choosing new players

foundation: a group that raises money for a cause

hat trick: three goals scored in a game by one person

point: a goal or an assist

postseason: another word for *playoffs*

rookie: a first-year player

stickhandle: to use a hockey stick to control the puck

LEARN MORE

Sports Illustrated Kids—Hockey
https://www.sikids.com/hockey

Anderson, Josh. *G.O.A.T. Hockey Centers.* Minneapolis: Lerner Publications, 2024.

Ice Hockey Facts for Kids
https://kids.kiddle.co/Ice_hockey

Mario Lemieux Foundation
https://mariolemieux.org/

Price, Karen. *Connor McDavid: Hockey Superstar.* Burnsville, MN: Press Box Books, 2020.

Scheff, Matt. *The Stanley Cup Finals: Hockey's Greatest Tournament.* Minneapolis: Lerner Publications, 2021.

INDEX

PHOTO ACKNOWLEDGMENTS

Jason Cohn/Icon SMI 764, p. 4; Andreas Hillergren/ZUMA Press/Newscom, p. 5; Spencer Lee/ZUMAPRESS/Newscom, p. 6; Perry Nelson-USA TODAY Sports, p. 7; Anna Krivitskaya/Shutterstock, p. 8; AP Photo/Gene J. Puskar, p. 9; AP Photo/Kevin Frayer, p. 10; AP Photo/John Swart, p. 11; Brendan Bannon/Polaris/Newscom, p. 13; Jason Franson/The Canadian Press via AP, p. 14; Jason Franson/The Canadian Press via AP, p. 15; AP Photo/Susan Walsh, p. 16; AP Photo/Paul Hurschmann, p. 17; Jean-Yves Ahern-USA TODAY Sports, p. 18; Sergei Belski-USA TODAY Sports, p. 19; AP Photo/Keith Srakocic, p. 20; IHA/Icon SMI 524/ IHA/Icon SMI/Newscom, p. 21; Charles LeClaire-USA TODAY Sports, p. 23; AP Photo/Keith Srakocic, p. 24; AP Photo/John Locher, p. 25; Perry Nelson-USA TODAY Sports, p. 26; Charles LeClaire-USA TODAY Sports, p. 27; AP Photo/Chris O'Meara, p. 28; Perry Nelson-USA TODAY Sports, p. 29.

Cover: Perry Nelson/Imagn/USA Today (Connor McDavid);
Tom Szczerbowski/Imagn/USA Today (Mario Lemieux).